Themis Aurea.

Laws of the Fraternity of the Rosy Cross

Count Michael Maierus,

Written in Latin by Count Michael Maierus, And now in English for the Information of those who seek after the knowledge of that Honourable and mysterious Society of wise and renowned Philosophers

Chapter I.

That all laws which bear the title of Themis, ought to respect their profit for whom they were made.

As laws do differ not only in their institutions, but their acceptance; so, if not tyrannically imposed, they Centre in the public good; for if by them humane society is maintained, Justice executed, virtue favoured, so that no man may fear the insolency and oppression of another, we may conclude that they profit and advance a Commonwealth: if every man duly receives whatever belongs to him, he hath no cause of commencing a suit with any, or to complain, much less to engage in a war; but on the contrary, all (as in the golden age) shall enjoy peace and prosperity, but the laws defend this justice by which only peace is established, contention ended, Themis worshipped, and lastly, all things in a flourishing state and condition. Whence the poets advisedly feigned Themis to be the daughter of heaven and earth, to be the sister of Saturn, and aunt to Jupiter, and have done her very much honour, and celebrated her fame, because she so constantly administered Justice: for equity and upright dealing were by her enjoyned, and all virtues which might render men either acceptable to the gods, or serviceable to each other, were to be embraced. She therefore taught them to live justly and contentedly, to shun violence, injuries and robbery; that they should ask nothing of the gods (as Festus observes) but what should favour of honesty and religion, or otherwise that their prayers would have no good issue. She furthermore said that the great God did look down upon the earth, and view the actions of men whether good or evil; and that he severely punished the wicked for their iniquity with eternal punishment; that he rewarded the good for their integrity with a life which shall neither end nor decay.

Others were of an opinion that this Themis was a prophetess amongst the Grecians, and did foretell what should happen, by which endowment she got great authority; so that they esteemed her an enthusiastess, and thought that she had familiarity with spirits, may even with the goddess themselves, from whom she sprung and had her original; to whom also after her decease she was supposed to have returned, where they have enlarged her Commission in relation to mankind. When she was accounted the goddess of justice, by her King's held their dominions; she instructed them in their duties to their subjects, and made the rude multitude pay due homage and subjection to their lawful Princes. She laid the foundations of magistracy and built an orderly structure of politics; for which cause she was in so high estimation amongst the heathens, that they supposed the world by her divinity to be upheld and supported. They erected temples to her, and instituted divine rites and ceremonies in honour of her. The first that was dedicated to her was in Boetia near to the river Cephissus, at which after the flood Ducalion and Pyrrha are said to have arrived; where they inquired of the oracle, how mankind which had perished in the deluge, might again be restored, as Ovid Liber primo.

O Themis, show what art it is that repairs,
Lost mankind, vouchsafed to help our sunk affairs.

This also was allegorically spoken concerning our Themis, that she being very prudent and more beautiful than all her contemporaries, was beloved of Jupiter; but after much sollicitation he was repulsed, and all intercourse broken off till at length she was surprised in Macedonia, and forced to be espoused to him, by whom she was with child, and brought forth three daughters; Equity, Justice, and Peace. She is reported to have had by the same Jupiter a son named Medius Fidius or the righteous, being faith's Guardian; wherefore an oath sworn by his name was sacred and unalterable: and this solemnity the Roman patriarchs challenged to themselves as their due, because it was held an execrable thing for an ingenious man to be fore-sworn.

Although we are confident that there was never upon the face of the earth any such Themis, who after consultation returned that oracle; much less that she was translated into heaven, as the heathens ignorantly imagined; yet we confess that the true idea of Justice, or an universal notion of virtue may herein (though occultly) be insinuated; for out of her springs good laws, and not as some think out of Vice, which is only a thing accidental.

This equity keeps kingdoms in safety, Commonwealths and cities in order, and lastly, improves small beginnings to a great height and degree of perfection.

This equity is that rule by which men ought to frame their words and actions. Polycletus a famous statuary made a book in which was proportionably expressed to the life each member in man's body, and he called this a pattern by which other artificers might examine and prove their pieces. Such rules indeed there are in all arts and sciences named axioms, which by deduction of things from their principles do rightly conclude.

This equity doth so poise all our manners and actions that they are not swayed to injustice and wickedness, whereby very many inconveniences are eschewed which happily might lead us away: for as luxury and riot are the causes of diseases, so injustice hath annexed to it as an inseparable companion loss and punishment: and on the contrary, as health renders men most happy, not only because of itself, but as it is big with other benefits: so by this equity, wholesome laws are enacted to the great comfort and advantage of mankind. But because this is so clear to every rational man, in vain are words spent to demonstrate it.

Chapter II.

Those laws which the founder of this Fraternity prescribed to the R. C. are all good and just.

As no rational man can deny the absolute necessity of good laws; so it is most fit that such laws should have their due praise and commendations; that the sluggard hereby might be pricked on to virtue, and the diligent might have his deserved reward.

Seeing therefore that these positions or laws, laid down by the father of the honourable Fraternity are worthy of special view, we shall truly according to their nature, and the advantages men may receive from them, Crown them with due commendations, counting them not only worthy of acceptance, but an Encomium.

First it is most reasonable that every society if it be good, should be governed by good laws; if otherwise, by bad: but that this society is good and lawful, we do not only suppose, but may gather from particular circumstances to which their positions are agreeable.

Something may be said concerning their number of 6, which hath very much of perfection in it; so that the society by an abundance of laws is not in confusion, nor yet by the paucity and fewness tied up from all liberty. When there are multitudes and great diversity of laws, we may probably conjecture that there will happen many crimes and enormities; for he that slighteth the straight path of Nature and reason, will certainly be misled into many windings and labyrinths before he comes to his journeys end. From these inconveniences our laws are free, as well in quality as number; they are voluntary, and such to whom all may easily assent as most rational.

They follow in their order.

1. That every one of them who shall travel, must profess medicine and cure gratis.
2. That none of them, notwithstanding their being of the fraternity, shall be enjoyned one habit; but may suit themselves to the custom and mode of those countries in which they reside.
3. That each brother of the Fraternity shall every year upon the day C. make his appearance in the place of the Holy spirit, are else signify by letters the true cause of his absence.
4. That every brother shall chose a fit person to be his successor after his decease.
5. That the world R.C. shall be their seal, character, or cognisance.
6. That this Fraternity shall be concealed an hundred years.

The brethren are solemnly sworn and strictly engaged to each other, to keep and observe these conditions and articles; in all which we find nothing either prejudicial to themselves, or hurtful and injurious to others; but that they have an excellent scope and intention, which is the glory of God and the good of their neighbour. We shall further prosecute these things, and by running through their several causes and circumstances, give any one a greater light into them.

In the first place, as touching the first author of these laws, it will be worthy our consideration to examine whether he had power and authority to make such laws for himself and others, and of requiring obedience thereto; then who was the author? And while his name hath been hitherto concealed?

It is most certain that a Prince who is as it were a head to his subjects that are his members, it is indeed a thing unquestionable, but that he hath full power of making and ratifying of laws: for chiefly it belongs to the Emperor, then to each King, because they have right to govern. Lastly it concerns any Princes or Civil magistrates.

But laws that are brought in by inferiours, extend only to those that have a particular relation to them; neither are they long lived, nor do they excuse from the laws of superiours, being only obligations which respect time, place, the person and subject.

Amongst the ancients those men who were of best repute for their wisdom, learning, authority, sincerity, and of greatest experiences, might set up laws in any city or nation. Thus we see that Moses was made regular and chieftain amongst the Hebrews, and amongst the heathen the first law-givers were called Zephyrians: after them Zaleucus in imitation of the Spartans and Cretians (who were thought to have received ancient laws from Minos) wrote severe laws, and found out suitable punishment; he left rules whereby men might try their actions, so that many afterwards were frighted into good manners; for before him laws were not written, but the sentence and state of the cause lay in the judge's breast.

Afterwards the Athenians received laws from Draco and Solon; upon which they proceeded in all courts of Judicature, from whom the Romans who lived after the building of the City three hundred years, had their laws of the twelve tables published by the Decemviri and these in process of time being enlarged by Roman magistrates and the Caesars, became our civil law which at this time is used amongst us.

Other nations also had their respective lawgivers, as Egypt had priests, and Isis, who were taught by Mercury and Vulcan. (These were golden laws, and such as owed their birth to the fire.) Babylon had the Caldeans, Persia had magicians, India had Brachmans, Ethiopia had the Gymnosophists; amongst the Bactrians was Zamolsis, amongst the Corinthians was Fido, amongst the Nilesians was Hippodamus, amongst the Carthaginians was Charonda, lastly amongst the Britons and French the Druids.

From what have already been said there may be gathered thus much, viz. that any one hath liberty (his companions complying and faithfully engaging) to prescribe laws to himself and them, especially if such laws are founded upon reason and equity; for (as the comedian has it) amongst the good ought to be transacted just and honest things; but as the combination of the wicked is unlawful, so are those bands that oblige them damnable, whose trust and fidelity are but true cheats and sure deceits; their constantly but obstinacy, their oaths cursings their rules methods of villany, their laws are commands to wickedness.

Our author indeed was a private man, and no magistrate; but in his particular relation he was invested with much authority, whereby he might oblige and bind others, be both Lord and Father of the society, and the first author and founder of this golden medicine and philosophical order. If any one shall attempt to usurp jurisdiction over against their wills and consent, he shall find his Labour to be in vain; for he must needs suppose them to have a prejudice against such designs, since he plays the bishop in another's Diocesse: but certainly the case is different here, because by a fair resignation they devoted themselves to his command.

Surely for confirmation we may take notice of the time; they have been kept and observed for many ages, and this doth not a little strengthen the first authority; for if you prescribe laws to any who were not under such before, and such laws continue a long season unviolated, it will follow that those laws being just and good may yet endure; for that nothing hinders, but that this private legislative power many be in force, being neither contrary to Divine or civil statutes, the laws of nature, any positive law, or custom of nations.

To some it may seem a strange thing that our author's name should not be known; to which we answer.

Our father indeed hath lain hid as being long since dead, and his brethren although they live and retain in record and memory his sacred name; yet because of some secret and weighty causes, are not willing to have his name or person known. Besides they have a continual succession and genealogy from him to themselves; and they received afterwards a lamp from a known confederate and colleague of their fraternity; they can read the author's soul in his books, view the true feature in the picture, Judge of the truth of the cause by the effect; whose actions confirm their goodness and sincerity; their hands are set with eyes, so that their belief goes beyond their sight; where other men foolishly and ignorantly think incredible and vain, they know how to be real and possible.

Shall we deny that those men who were chosen and selected to be of the fraternity, were unacquainted with our author? Surely they were most intimate and familiar with him, and performed with alacrity whatever he commanded or enjoined them.

To those indeed to whom the knowledge of him was no benefit, he was not, neither was it necessary that he should be known, unless such persons over curious pried into matters which concern them not, for as it belongs not to us to have intelligence what designs are in agitation within the walls of Troy, or who in India doth administer justice or give laws; so likewise ought they not to intermeddle with this author and his brethren altogether unknown to them. If we behold smoke breathing out of an House, we presently concluded that there is fire within. And why should not we although the father and the fraternity have not been seen by outward eye, yet because of their works, by the eye of our minds discern and satisfy ourselves concerning them? We can pass a judgement upon a tree by the fruit, although the fruit be plucked off; it suffices to the knowledge of a man if we hear him speak: whence Socrates spake thus to a young virtuous man, but one that held his peace; speak (said he) that I may hear thee. A dog discovers himself by his Barking, a Nightingale by her sweet chanting notes; and we judge of all other things according to their actings. And why then cannot we distinguish this our author from cheats by his positions and laws, since it is the others whole design to delude? They make gain of their tricks; that which would be irksome to another, they take pleasure in, and make a sport of dangers and hazards.

Our author is nameless, but yet worthy of credit, unknown to the vulgar, but well known to his own society. And some may ask the reason of his concealment. We know that the ancient philosophers counted themselves happy in a private life; and wily may not moderns enjoy the same privilege, since necessity may put these more upon it than them? The world is now more burdened with wickedness and impieties: indeed the whole creation as it flowed from God was exceedingly good, but man's fall have brought a curse upon the creatures. Polidorus had not been so credulous, could he have foreseen his fate; by whose example others have got wisdom, they dare not entrust themselves with the rude multitude, but secretly do withdraw themselves; for commonly an handsome opportunity makes a thief; and he that exposes his treasures upon a high hill to all means eyes, invites robbers. Men called Homines have both their name and nature ab humo, from the earth, which sometimes been parched with extreme heat opens; sometimes seems to be drowned with floods; which depend upon the Sun, wind, showers, either of them either yielding no influence at all, or exceeding in their operations. Even so the mind of man is not always in the same condition; sometimes it enlarges itself in covetousness, sometimes Vice is more pleasing to its than virtue, and plundering is preferred before honesty and justice. But I would not be thought to include all men in this censure; for we intend only those who having neither reason not learning, to differ very little from the brute beasts.

Wherefore the father of this fraternity was not so much careful of concealing himself in respect of his own interest; but herein he wisely consulted the good and welfare of his successors and the whole fraternity. Shall we esteem him a wise man who is not wise for himself? So that Aristippus, Anaxarchus and many others do worthily bear their disgraces. Everyone by dangerous achievements and noble exploits can get renown; and some have grown famous by notorious and execrable villanies; as Herostratus who fired the great temple of Diana: but this our author and his successors conceal themselves, very well knowing what a sting, honour and popularity carries in the tail of it; not that they hate or scorn human society, but that they may as it were at a distance behold the enormities of men, being only spectators and not actors. Democritus is reported to have put out his eyes that he might not see the vanity and emptiness of the world in respect of goodness and virtue, and its fullness of deceit, luxury and all Vice: but our author and his successors have taken a very wise course to conceal themselves: no man that would exactly see an object, will fix both his eyes upon it; neither will a wise man put himself into the hands of either Mercury or Mars, they being patrons of thieves and robbers; neither will he entrust himself with Jupiter or Apollo since that the one is armed with thunderbolts, the other with arrows, by which the unfortunate Hyacinthus perished, and was metamorphosed into a flower bearing his name.

Chapter III.

Concerning the general intent and effect of these laws with the particular circumstances of place, time, means, and the end.

We have already at large discoursed of the maker and efficient cause of these laws; now we shall treat of their effects and circumstances.

That is probably termed an effect which in all points agrees with its cause: so that if our author was an upright man, these laws which flow from him shall likewise be good, it being a very rare thing to see a virtuous offspring degenerate from their parents and ancestors.

It is evident enough that these laws do answer their intention, by that order and firm knot of friendship which yet continues amongst that Honourable Society; for if reason, Nature, and truth, had not justified their proceedings, doubtless they had long since been ruined and come to nothing. Many indeed aim well, but yet hit not the mark; and we know that a sudden storm crosses the endeavour and desire of the mariner in arriving at his safe haven: even so he that sets himself to any noble exploit, shall find blocks in his way; and if he goes through with it, God should have due thanks by whose Providence and blessing he obtains so happy an issue.

Hitherto these brethren have not repented of their condition, neither will they ever, being servants to the king of kings, all the fruits of their labours they dedicate to him. Religion with them is in greater esteem than any thing in the world; as well in the book of Nature as the written word they read and study God's omnipotency, his providence and his mercy; they account it their duty to help and relieve the poor and oppressed; and surely such actions become Christians; so unworthy a thing it is that heathens and Turks should out-stripe us in them!

It is not necessary that any should know their place of meeting, but they whom it properly concerns. We are sure that it is not in Utopia, or amongst the Tartars, but by chance in the middle of Germany; for Europe seems to resemble a virgin, and Germany to be her belly; it is not decent that a virgin should discover herself, lest she rather be accounted a strumpet than a Virgin: let it suffice that we know her not to be barren; to have conceived, yea and brought forth this happy Fraternity: although hers is a virgin womb, yet she have teemed with many rare and unknown arts and sciences. We mean Germany which at present flourishes and abounds with roses and lilies, growing in philosophical gardens where no rude hand can crop or spoil them.

The Hesperian nymphs have their abode here Aegle, Heretusa and Hespretusa, with their golden boughs, lest they again become a prey to Hercules, are here secured. Here are Geryons vast bulls in fair and safe pasture, neither Cacus, nor any malicious person can steal or persecute them. Who can deny that the golden fleece is here, or the princely garden of Mars and Aeta who is feigned to be the son of Phoebus and Phaeton's brother? Here are fed the sheep and oxen of the Sun called

Pecudes, whence is derived the word Pecunia, money, the Queen of the world.

It would be to no purpose to speak of the means by which these things have been deduced from their first author; since that the brethren in their book entitled their Fame and Confession, and in other writing have at large declared them. He brought them first from Arabia into Germany his native country, and then designed to make up the Fraternity; and these made the first part of the book called M of which there is so much mention in their Fama; which was afterwards translated out of Arabic into Latin; out of which book M they learned many mysteries, and in it as in a glass they clearly saw the anatomy and idea of the universe: and doubtless shortly they will let the book M come abroad into the world, that those who covet after knowledge may receive satisfaction: nay I confidently believe that happy day to be at hand; so we may judge of the Lion by his paw; far as the ebbings and flowings of the Sea (as Basil Valentine reports) doth carry much wealth to diverse kingdoms; so these secrets coming into public view, having much in them of the worlds harmony so much admired by Pythagoras, may yield us no less profit and content.

Neither hath it been ever known that two have been so much alike as this to the M yes this F is the M neither must we expect another M.

The end for which these laws were made was the common good and benefit which partly belongs to the brethren themselves, and partly respects others, either in their minds or bodies to the furnishing of that with knowledge, and to the remedying of the diseases of the other, for they being ambitious to profit and advantage others, have taken a course suitable to their intentions.

But if any shall object and say that they have not consulted their own safety, these things will confute; as also that they have endeavoured the good and welfare of others.

In this case the scales hang very even, inclining neither to the one nor other, and the first Unity is equivalent to the fifth, or second and third linked together; every one (as the proverb hath it) will christen his own child first; and rivers (as the wise man speaks) stream not out, unless the fountain is full; he gives best, that gives so to one that he may give oftentimes.

But when were these laws first promulgated, you may learn out of the Fama by chance about the year 1413! If he was born in the year 1378 and travelled at 16 years of age, he was out six years, and returned at the end of eight but expected five years before he brought his business to any end, and gave his laws: but these things are rather conjectural than certain, in regard that we want the history in which they are distinctly set down.

Chapter IV.

Of the first Law and the excellency of Medicine above all other Arts to which the Brethren are devoted.

We are now come to treat more particularly of each Law, and we will begin with the first, viz.

That whoever of them shall travel, must profess Medicine and cure gratis without any reward.

Necessity hath forced men to invent Arts for their help; curiosity hath set others on to work to satisfy fancy; and luxury hath not been idle in seeking out means to please itself. Now amongst these arts and inventions, some are more noble and excellent, both in respect of themselves and in the estimation of men. Do not we count it a Divine and majestical thing to govern? What more glorious than to wage war with success? There are merchants, handycraftsmen and husbandmen in a commonwealth, and every one acts in his proper sphere. In any profound points in divinity we consult the able clergy; in a doubtful and subtile case we go to an able and honest lawyer; in desperate sickness we seek to an experienced and learned physician. But Medicine deservedly seems to have pre-eminence; for a physician in sickness governs the Emperor, prescribes rules and directions which the lawyer cannot do, for the law-giver being present, the law has no force, and may be changed and altered at his pleasure who first instituted them.

The physician likewise fights with the diseases of man's body and hath sharp battles with them; he overcomes to the preserving or restoring health almost lost and decayed. Hence Aristotle places health amongst those things in which all men agree; for everyone knows that it is best and desires to be well and in the next place to be rich and wealthy.

Wherefore a physician's employment is so far from being contemptible, that it is concerned in a man's chiefest outward good and happiness, in maintaining health and curing diseases. God at first created man. Nature, God's handmaid, conduceth to the generation of him from the seed of both sexes; and it is the physician's office to recover man diseased, and to restore him to his native health. So that this Art hath much in it of divinity, having the same subject with the creation and generation, viz., Man, who being created after the image of God was His by creation, being begotten was Nature's by generation; nay Christ himself being incarnate did not disdain to be as well as the physician of the Soul, so also to be the physician of the body. The prophets among the Israelites practised physick, the priests among the Egyptians, out of whose number the Kings were chosen. Lastly great princes have studied this Art, not covetously for the reward, but that they might help the sick. We have heard of some who having slain many in a just war, yet to cleare themselves have freely given physick, doing good to me to expiate the hurt they had formerly done.

Wherefore since the profession of physick is so high, so noble and sacred, we need not admire that amongst other arts and sciences in which they excel, these Brethren of the Honourable Society should choose and prefer this above them all. I confidently believe that they, knowing the most intimate secrets of Nature, can naturally produce very strange effects, which as much amaze an ignorant spectator as the Gorgon's head, but Medicine was dearer to them, as being of most profit and greater value.

But some, perhaps, may exclaim against the Brethren, saying that they are not physicians, but mere empirics, who intrude upon physick. Such, indeed, should first look at home and then abroad. I confess that few of the Brethren have had their education, but yet they are great scholars, not fresh or raw in profound learning, but the greatest proficients. They compound that Medicine which they administer, it being, as it were, the marrow of the Great World.

To speak yet more plainly, their Medicine is Prometheus his fire, which, by the assistance of Minerva, he stole from the Sun and conveyed it unto man; although diseases and maladies were afterwards by the Gods (as the poets feign) inflicted on men, yet the balsam of Nature was more powerful than the distempers. This fire was spread over all the world, conducing to the good both of body and mind, in freeing the one from infirmities, the other from grievous passions; for nothing doth more cheer and make glad the heart of man than this Universal Medicine. Precious stones wrought into subtile powder and leaf gold are the ingredients of this powder, commonly called Edel heriz Pulver. Aeschylus doth attribute the invention of pyromancy, the composition of Medicines, the first working upon Gold, Iron and other metals to Prometheus; hence the Athenians erected an altar common to him, Vulcan and Pallas, considering how much fire conduced to the finding out of the secrets of Nature. But we must know that a four-fold fire is required to bring this Medicine to perfection, and if one of them is wanting, the whole labour is lost.

Chapter V.

That the cure of diseases by specific remedies of occult quality, which the Fraternity useth, is most suitable to man's nature and prevalent against all distempers.

We must not by what hath been hitherto spoken suppose that the Brethren use Medicines which are not natural, for they have vegetables and minerals, but they, having a true knowledge of the secret and occult operation of things, know what will be most effectual for their purpose.

They have their Panchresta, their Polychresta, their Manus Christi, and other great titles; their Narcotica and Alexipharmaca, of which Galen and others do much boast, thinking them a present help at a dead lift; and to colour their cheats, strictly command that none shall either prescribe or give them without a large fee, as if the price added virtue to them and the effect did much depend upon the cost.

The Brethren also have variety of Medicines; some called Kings, some Princes, some nobles and others knights, each one being denominated according to its excellence and worth. But we must take notice that they prescribe not according to the purse, but the infirmity of the patient; neither do they desire a reward beforehand; they likewise fit not a child's shoe to an old man, because a due proportion ought to be carefully observed; a dram is sufficient for the one, and an ounce of the same Medicine for the other. Who would not think it absurd to apply the same plaster to the hardened and brawny hand of a ploughman and to the delicate and neat hand of a scholar or gentleman?

He that practiseth Physick aright doth consider the different temper of persons in the same disease, as a learned judge doth not always give the same judgement in the same cause, which circumstances may very much alter. The Brethren look chiefly to the constitution of the patient and do accordingly prescribe.

They have in all things experience to confirm their knowledge; they use very choice vegetables, which they gather when they are impregnated with heavenly influences, not deluded with common, idle Astrological notions, but certainly knowing at what time they have received a signature effectual to such an end; and they apply these vegetables to such diseases for which they were intended.

It is a most irrational thing when Nature hath afforded us simple Medicines to correct and amend their deficiencies, that we should mix and compound with qualities hot, cold, moist and dry, so that one specific being, perhaps secretly of a contrary operation to another ingredient, the proper virtues of both, if not lost, yet are much diminished.

The Galenists say that the first qualities do alter, that the second do either thicken or attenuate, and so foolishly and ignorantly of the rest; whereas each vegetable hath in it virtue essentially to chase away that disease in which it may rightly be applied. It is here in Medicine as in an Army; if each soldier falls out with the other or they mutiny against their commander, the enemy gets strength and makes use of their weapons to slay them.

Some may ask what is here meant by Specific? I answer that I intend that which the illiterate Galenists calls an occult quality, because it is neither hot, cold, moist or dry; because indeed true profound knowledge was above their reach or understanding.

Valescus de Taranta, lib. 7, cap. 12, defines the Galenical occult quality. A question is started how a locust hanged about the neck doth cure a Quartain? To which they answer, that if these empirical Medicines have any such virtue, they have it from their occult quality, which contains the specific form of the distemper conjoined with the influence of the Stars. But then we may ask what that total propriety is? Averrhoes calls it a complexion; others say that it is the substantial form of a compound body; some will have it to be the whole mixture, viz., the form, the matter and complexion, which Avicenna names the whole substance, when he said that a body hath neither operation from the matter, nor quality, but the whole substance or composition.

But to speak truely and clearly as it becomes Philosophers, we hold that there is a natural virtue and certain predestination flowing from the influence of heavenly bodies, so particularly disposing the form to be introduced, that it is (as it were) determined to its proper object, whereby after due preparation of the matter, and conjunction of the form, the whole substance or mixed body necessarily produces a proportionable effect. And Avicenna perhaps meant thus much; whence Arnoldus, in his book De Causis Sterilitatis, saith that the peculiar property of a thing is its nature which proceeds from the right disposition of the parts to be mixed, and this is called an occult quality, to most men unknown because of its difficulty. Hence it is that Nature is styled a complexion, not because it is so properly, and found out by reason, its secrets being only discovered by experiment and practice; by this the understanding knows that experience is above reason; because there are so many experiments of which we can give no rational account, nor find out any method to satisfy ourselves concerning them.

By what hath hitherto been spoken, it plainly appears that the whole propriety of anything is not the complexion; for if it were so, all things which have the same propriety, would consequently have the same complexion, which is false; for Rhubarb and Tamarinds, from their whole propriety do attract and draw choler, and yet are not of the same complexion. Thus Valescus.

It is therefore evident that the true propriety of medicinal things is only known by experiment, and not by the false Galenical rules of Art, which do not give us light into the nature of any simple. For instance, consider the Rose, it sends forth a most pleasant perfume and is of a ruddy lovely colour, not in respect of the quality cold and dry, but of that proper virtue essentially in it; neither can there be any deduction from these qualities, being not subject to taste, to feeling, to hearing and consequently none at all, because specifics have another original.

How are the first qualities observed? Not from their essence and nature, but as sense discovers them, whence reason draws a conclusion: But we see not how reason can determine concerning the qualities of a rose, whether it is hot, cold, moist and dry, unless it hath been informed by the senses as by the colour, scent, taste or touch.

But these rules are altogether uncertain and fallacious, and there are more experiments to overthrow then to confirm them; for who dare affirm that all cold things can have no scent; that all hot things have scent? That all scented things are hot; that all that have no scent are cold; or that white things are cold or hot; that red things are hotter than white; or contrarily that bitter things are hot, narcotic cold etc.? For opium, the Spirit of Wine, the Rose and more things will confute such an opinion, so that the qualities do depend upon such uncertainties in respect of every simple, that it is far better to trust to experience, to search into the secrets of Nature, than vainly to trifle away time in gathering the second qualities from the first, and the third from the second, or to gain reason by sense, a thing most ridiculous unless it be in the cure of diseases, where the qualities are in confusion.

When the Egyptians understood this they studied and most esteemed of that physick which was experimental and not notional, and therefore they used to place their sick persons in the streets, that if any one of the people that passed by had laboured under the same disease, he might tell the specific remedy with which he was cured; whence it sometimes falls out that an old woman or an empiric in some certain diseases may effect more by one proper specific than many physicians by their methods and long courses.

I would not be misunderstood, as if there were no judgement to be used in the administration of physick, but that experience should be the only guide. Medicine, whether speculative or practical, must concur and meet in truth. I say we must not, as to the invention or prescription of physick, trust too much to reason enformed falsely and concerning the nature of things, but when experience hath confirmed us in mysteries and secrets, because reason is too weak-sighted to teach them, we must not perversely slight them, disesteeming enviously what we cannot attain.

I do not account him a rational physician who hath only a large scroll or bill of simples in his memory, and can distinctly tell you what are hot in the first degree, what in the second, what in the third, and can run through the second qualities and third; and if at any time he is called to a patient, from this rabble, as from the belly of the Trojan horse, issue many receipts, many bands, when he is ignorant of the most inconsiderable simple, and knows not how rightly to apply it. Shall not he who understands and is well acquainted with his Medicines, be of more repute? A few select prescriptions that are infallible and effectual to the cure are of more worth than a rude multitude of Galenical receipts.

We have, indeed, now so great a variety of Medicines that it puzzles a physician more to choose what is best than to invent; for it is not the abundance of remedies that overcomes a disease, but the virtue, method, order and choice of time and place that give success.

We read in histories of the courage and skill of a Spartan King, who, with a band of four hundred stout Lacedemonians, possessed the straights by which Xerxes should pass with an army of one million, seven hundred thousand and made there a great slaughter of them. When the insulting Persian boasted that they would close the Sun with their arrows, the Spartan King answered that then we will fight in the shadow.

By these examples it appears that a select company of choice soldiers have great advantage against a confused multitude. And why are not a few choice remedies beyond a heap of vain receipts? Some have said that an army is complete that hath an hundred thousand, and if the number exceeds, it will be tumultuous and in no order and discipline. We may assert the like of Medicine, if it increaseth to a great number it rather kills than cures; for every specific waging war or being opposite to another, must necessarily disturb Nature's peace and tranquillity.

Chapter VI.

Although other Physicians may challenge, as indeed they deserve, a due reward, yet the Brethren do cure gratis, not valuing money.

We read in history that great persons, Kings and Princes, have entertained famous and learned physicians, not only allowing them a considerable annual stipend, but have raised them to great preferment and honour. Eristratus found out the disease of Antiochus, viz. his love of his mother in law, of which he recovered him and received of his son Ptolemy one hundred talents. Democides restored the tyrant Polycrates for two talents of Gold. The same person, for curing Darius, had given to him a very rich chain of Gold and two golden cups. Jacobus Cocterius, physician to Louis the second, King of France, had fifty thousand crowns yearly paid to him and Thaddeus the Florentine got fifty crowns daily, travelling up and down to cure the sick.

The rewards and gains physick bringeth in hath caused many students to employ all their time and labour therein, who for the most part look more to the profit than health of their neighbour, and good of the commonwealth. If we indeed consider to how many infirmities we are subject, we shall find physick to be as necessary as food and raiment, and then able physicians are to be sought for, who may judiciously administer it; but no man will employ all his pains, cost and labour, in that of which he shall reap no harvest; Who will be another's servant for no wages? Will a lawyer plead without his fee? Neither is there any injunction or law to command and oblige a Doctor to cure for nothing. It would be very hard and rigorous, if any man should be forced to give away what should properly belong to him. Menecrates the Syracusan had nothing for his pains, but affected divinity; he would be thought and accounted Jupiter, which was worse than if he had required a reward suitable to his calling.

The Brethren are so far from receiving a fee that they scorn it; so far from vain glory of their success, that they will not have such a favour acknowledged. They have not one Medicine for a great man, another for the poor, but equally respect both; frequent in visiting, comforters in affliction and relievers of the poor. Their labour is their reward, their pains to them gain; no mice or other vermin can diminish their heap, no Dragon or wild beast can either poison or exhaust their fountain.

Coelius, lib. 16, cap. 10, tells us of Philo, a physician, who found out certain Medicines which he called The Hands of the Gods; but this great title was but as ivy hung out for a show to take the eyes of the spectators, to surprise the ears of the hearers, which promised more than they performed and rather deluded than helped any, having a glorious outside, but within dregs and corrupt. But the Brethren, although they have the most efficacious Medicines in the world, yet they had rather conceal the virtues than boast of them. Their powders perhaps may be accounted a little Cinnabar or some slight stuff, but they effect more than seems to be expected from them. They possess the Phalaia and the Asa of Basileus; the Nepenthes that drives away sorrow of Homer and

Trismegistus; the ointment of Gold; the fountain of Jupiter Hammon, which at night is hot, at noon is cold, lukewarm at sun rising and setting. For they condemn gains and income by their possession, neither are they enticed with honour or preferment, they are not so overseen as one of whom Tully speaks, who wrote against others affectation of esteem and placed his name in the frontispiece of his book that he might be more known; they embrace security and are not buried, but live and are active in silence.

Is not this a rare society of men who are injurious to none, but seek the good and happiness of all, giving to each person what appertains to him? These Brethren do not adore the rising Sun, mere parasites who conform themselves to the becks of great men; their words and actions are masked with cheats.

It is reported that the statue of Diana by art was so framed that if a present was brought her by a pilgrim, she would show a cheerful and pleasing countenance, but if anyone came empty she frowned, was angry and seemed to threaten. Even so is the whole world, wherein all things are subject to Gold. This dust of the earth is of no value with them, because these things are low in their eyes, which others most adore. They had rather find out a mystery in nature than a mine, and as Gold serves to help forward their studies, so they esteem of it. They wish and are ambitious of the age of Solomon, wherein there was so great plenty at Jerusalem as tiles on the houses, Silver as common as stones in the Street; so in the Golden Age its use was not known; men were contented with what Nature freely afforded them, living friendly under the government of the father of the family, without broils, luxury, pride, much less war.

Chapter VII.

Abuses in Medicine censured, as the long Bills for ostentation, that the Physician may not seem an Empirick, and for the Apothecaries gain, without respect to the benefit and purse of the diseased, when a few choice simples might do the cure.

We daily see how many weeds sprung from Gold, have and do still overrun the whole world. It hath not only overthrown cities, destroyed commonwealths, but also hath corrupted the Arts, and of liberal hath made them almost servile.

Let us a little (passing by the rest) cast our eyes upon Medicine, whose streams the further they have run from the fountain, the more dirt and mire they have drunk up; and now at last they are full of stench and filthiness. We before have said that Nature is contented with a little, which holds good as well in sickness as in health, for the more simple diet is, the easier it is digested, because it is hard to turn many heterogeneous things into one substance. So likewise in diseases, the variety of ingredients distracts, if not totally hinders Nature in her operation, in regard she struggles not only with the infirmity but the very remedy; and how can those things which are opposite and fight among themselves procure and maintain peace?

We confess that a judicious composition is necessary, because one simple specific cannot confer to the cure of complicated distempers, so that more simples united may effect that which one could not: neither would we be thought so absurd as to question so good and requisite a method.

That which we complain of is the great multitude of omnium gatherum put together of herbs, roots, seeds, flowers, fruits, barks, hot or cold in the first, second and third degree; so that you shall have thereby forty or more ingredients in one receipt, to show the memory and art of a dull and blockish physician, and to help the knavish apothecary, who extols his gain for learnedness, the quick utterance of his drugs for experimental knowledge.

On the contrary, if anyone making conscience of what he undertakes shall prescribe a few rare and approved simples (as that famous Crato did, physician to three Caesars) he shall be thought an ignoramus, if not a mere empiric, although he excel those receipt-mongers by far in all parts of learning.

Take notice how the apothecaries slight a short though effectual bill, because it brings in little profit; but if they receive a bill of a cubit long, they bless themselves and thus the patient pays for his sickness, when, if he recovers, his purse will be sick.

Consider how injurious these are to each person and the commonwealth; by destroying the one they diminish the other; for if they remain, yet are they but poor members thereof. The disease is protracted by the contrariety of Medicines and Nature weakened. We account it absurd when a straight way leads to the wood, for haste to countermarch and make windings which may confound and not further. Multitude breeds in most things confusion, but especially in Medicine, when the essences of simples are not known.

We may fetch examples to confirm this from a Court, where if everyone at the same time may plead and declare his opinion, the case would be made more intricate, so far would they be from deciding the controversy. Wherefore a few wise counsellors on each side will clearly state the case and bring it to a sudden and safe determination. The same discord will appear in physick, if each simple in the same disease should have its operation, when a few select ones may quickly do the business.

It is therefore an expedient course out of many things to choose a few, out of those that are good to pick the best, which may assist and strengthen Nature in her conflict. If these observations were taken notice of, a physician would not be reputed able for his large, rude bills, but for the quality of his ingredients; the apothecary would have more custom, because men would not be frightened with the charge and die to save expenses, but willingly submit to an easy and honest cure.

Everything is not to be esteemed according to its bulk; we see that brute beasts in body and quantity exceed a man, but yet the lesser, being rational and wise, doth govern the other. A little Gold is worth more than a heap of stones, than a mine of base metals; so in Medicine a small quantity may have more virtue in it than a great measure of many simples.

It is sufficiently known to wise men, that the same herbs do alter under several climates; and that which is innocent in one may be poison in another; wherefore it is not safe to compound India, Arabia, America, Germany and England together, for the Sun and planets have a different influx upon this or that country and accordingly alter the plants. Nay we cannot be ignorant that the same field abounds, as with wholesome, so with venomous herbs; we have example of this truth in minerals, for common Salt alone is harmless, as also our vulgar Mercury; but if these two be sublimed together, they become a venomous and rank poison; but perhaps some may think that this proceeds from Mercury, which indeed is false, for it may be brought by Art to run again, and then its innocency returns. So likewise the Spirit of Vitriol may be taken without danger, mixed with another liquor, and the water of Saltpeter may be received into the body, but if these two be distilled together, they make a water that will eat any metal except Gold and certain death to anyone that shall take it. But if you add to the former Armoniack, its strength is increased and it will reduce Gold into a watery and fluid substance, yet its nature is pure and perfect.

It may be objected that Treacle, Mithridate, and confection of Hamech, with others, were compounded of many simples, which being after long fermentation well digested, became most sovereign remedies and have been in use almost six hundred years and have helped many thousands of people.

We deny not but these compositions are excellent and have been in great esteem in foregoing and latter ages; we likewise approve perhaps of six hundred more, if they are grounded upon experience. For they who first invented these Medicines did not consider whether the qualities were hot or cold, but to their nature and essence as they either resisted poison or conduced to the evacuation of ill humors in the body, as in Treacle there is vipers flesh and many others of the same virtue. Our discourse is against the vain, extemporary ostentation in prescribing of Medicines compounded of plants hot, dry, cold and moist, either in this or that degree.

We knew a physician who was wont to boast that he knew not any one particular experiment, but all remedies were alike to him, respective the first, second and third qualities: and this surely proceeded from his ignorance of what was to be known; but a wise and prudent spirit searches more narrowly and descends to particulars. For indeed it is more easy by general rules to pass a judgement of simples, than by experience to find out the proper virtue of specifics; and the reason is because each simple hath a peculiar property which distinguisheth it from another and sometimes contrary; nay the qualities do not only differ in respect of others, but the same simple may have effects differing in itself as it appears in Rhubarb, which in respect of its first qualities, hot and dry, it doth increase choler in man's body, but in respect of its essence and specific nature it purgeth it. To pass by Opium and Vinegar, with many others, we see how the same thing in their first second and third qualities have many times contrary operations; so Rennet makes thin thickened blood of the hare, but if it be very fluid it thickens it; so also Vitriol, according to its nature, doth penetrate and is astringent, yet it doth repel and disperse lead outwardly applied to it; though Quicksilver is most weighty, yet by the fire it is sublimed and ascends and though it is a thick, gross body, it may by Art be made to pierce any body and afterwards be reduced to its own native purity.

Many more proofs might be brought, for there is nothing in the world, how abject and low soever, but it hath a stamp upon it as a sure seal of its proper virtues, of which he that is ignorant hath hitherto attained but the husk and shell, the outside of knowledge.

Lest therefore this error in judgement should corrupt practice, and men's lives thereby should be in danger, we thought is a good piece of service to desire those who bend and employ their studies in the honorable faculty of Medicine, to seek more after a few rare and certain specifics, than to follow generals which so commonly deceive. We ought not to show ourselves so impious and undutiful, as being in honour, having encrease of riches, to scorn our poor parents; so experience is the mother of Art; and shall we now condemn her as having no need of her? Experience has been stiled the Mistress of Fools, and Reason the Queen of wise men; but in a different respect they ought not to be separated, as many experiments beget reason, so reason maintains and adorns experience.

Chapter VIII.

That many Medicines, because of their high titles, and the fond opinion of men who think that best which costs most, are in great esteem; though others of less puce, proper to the Country, are far above them in excellency and worth.

Besides the abuses mentioned in the foregoing chapter, another is crept in; the former were cheats in respect of quantity and quality; here by this the purse is emptied; for they fall in with men's humours, who think a thing good when they have well bought it.

Hence Galen concealed his Golden Emplaister for the Squinancy, by which he got an hundred crowns, which indeed was in itself of little worth; for there are many things of excellent use which if they were divulged, would be foolishly despised, because vulgar hands pollute whatever comes into them. Some reason may be why after they are not so successful, because the imagination and fancy works not so strongly, and desponds as to the cure from such slight means and so hinders the operation; for although another man's imagination hath little force upon me, yet mine own much alters the body and either hinders or furthers a remedy in its working.

As this is clear in many diseases, so especially in hypocondriac melancholy, called the shame of physicians because rarely cured, wherein the non-effecting of the cure depends upon the prejudiced imagination of the patient, who despairs of help; for cares, grief and despair, do alter and change the blood, corrode the heart, overwhelm the spirits that they cannot perform their offices; if therefore these can first be removed, there is very great hope of recovery.

Under this cloak many cover their knavery and covetousness, who seek nothing but gain by their practice; for they call their Medicines by great names, that the imagination of the patient, closing with so rich and precious remedies, may promote the cure; and therefore they compound their Medicines of rare ingredients as Gold, Silver, Pearls, Bezoar, Ambergris, Musk and many more, and then they christen them according to their birth. They call them the Balsam of Life, the Great Elixir, the Restorative of Life, Potable Gold, Butter and Oil of the Sun; and who indeed can reckon up their tricks by which they draw in and delude such multitudes of ignorant people? Yet their great names are not altogether insignificant; for by this Balsam of Life they mean that which maintains and keeps themselves alive.

But grant these costly Medicines to be good and useful, yet they must confess that others not so chargeable have greater virtues in them.

We may also question whether they deal honestly and do not sell a little Salt for Gold and rank poison for the Balsam of Life; we have known some at death's door by their Mercury. I speak this that others may be cautious. Think what would come of it when one mistaking administered Opium for Apium or parsley. Thus they try experience upon men's bodies and kill one to save another.

Besides, though these may be very excellent cordials or antidotes, yet are they not appropriated to the disease, and so consequently little conducing to the grief.

Consider, then, the abuse; the patient pays a great price for that which is of small advantage to him and scorns those means which are at an easy rate, wherein also there is no danger, as being by experience confirmed and by all hands received.

It is not hard to prove that each country abounds with simples suitable to the diseases of that country, and that we need not go to India or use exotic drugs.

This question has been handled by many learned men; at present we will not spend much time about it. We deny not the use in food and physick of India[n] and Arabic spices, neither do we condemn other most excellent gifts of God; but here we find fault with the price. Let us, therefore, use them in their place and time. Perhaps such precious things were intended for great persons, but yet great care must be used in the preparation that they be not sophisticated. I say rich men may afford to pay for these Medicines, who delight to eat and drink Gold, and hope as by that they can purchase all earthly things, so they may buy health.

Neither would we be thought ignorant of the great virtues and efficacy of Gold, but we speak against the abuse of those imposters who instead thereof do cheat and rob: and we can assure all that there is no worth in the boiling and reboiling of Gold. They indeed give their menstruous stuffs for dissolved Gold, which, being reduced to a Spirit, may corrode (and let all men beware of it); imitating a careless cook, who if he hath lost the broth in which the meat hath been boiled sets now upon the table which hath no heart nor strength in it. So they, when they have consumed and lost their Gold with Salts and other ways, they sell that which remains. When the bird is gone they sell the nest, and this they call Potable Gold, spiritualised because invisible. It may be they put Gold into their furnace, but that they by those means can produce such Medicines we deny. There were many Alexanders, many called by the name of Julius, but yet but one Alexander the Great, one Julius Caesar; the others agree only in name.

Should anyone enquire into the excellency of our own countries simples, he would have work enough upon his hands. We shall leave this to another time and place.

But besides the price, may we not justly suspect the preparation; that they, instead of true, may well sell false compositions, failing in their art and profession? For the balance of human frailty being at the one end by justice, at the other by profit, the last overweighs; because honesty may be an hindrance to us, but profit brings pleasure and delight along with it. So now merchants count it part of their trade to learn and skill the adulterating of their commodities. When the Thebans would admit no such persons to the magistracy, unless they had left off their trade at least ten years before, by which time they might forget to cozen; but I will not here censure all of that calling. The same may be said of those who sell Medicines, whether physicians or apothecaries, if they abuse their profession.

It remains to show that specifics or vegetables and things of little worth, are more powerful against any disease than those which are of so great price; neither is the reason fetched far; for they whose property absolutely resists the malady, they (I say) must needs be more effectually than those who accidentally suit the disease, and by mere chance work a cure. In mechanic arts if a man excellent in one should boast of his skill in another which he never saw, you would find him a bungler in it, but employ the same in that trade wherein he hath been brought up and he will show himself to be a workman; so in diseases, when each specific doth its own office there is a happy issue, but applied to another proves of no effect. Neither can it be expected from one man (though he had an hundred hands) to conquer an army, which yet choice bands of experienced soldiers may easily overcome; but we have been tedious about this subject.

Chapter IX.

That many are haters of Chymistry, others scorn the use of vegetables and Galenical compositions, either of which may be useful in proper cases.

As the palates of men are not all taken with the same taste, but what is pleasing to one, is loathsome to another, so men's judgements differ, and what one approves the other assents not unto, both which happen or are caused as by sympathy or antipathy, drawing them on to embrace, and provoking them to hate such a thing; so also by prejudice or reason corrupted.

Some dare not taste cheese all their life, some abstain from it for a few years, some drink only water, refusing wine or ale; and in these there is great variety. No less is the difference amongst minds, whence it is that two meeting when neither hath seen or heard of the other, at the first sight, shall desire and seek each other's friendship; and, on the contrary, whence is it that one hates another from whom he hath never received injury? as evidently appears by one coming where two are gaming, he presently shall find his affection to close with the one, and if his wish might succeed he should win, and he would gladly have the other lose, though he neither received courtesy from the one, nor harm or ill word from the other.

Now as much as the understanding excels the taste and dull and sensual faculty, so much a truly wise man surpasseth one that only outwardly seems judicious. One by reflection considers and weighs the matter, the other not so acutely apprehending is tempted to rashness. Thus many learned men, whose fancies have not been in due subjection to their understandings, have abused themselves and have heedlessly embraced this as good and cast off that as evil.

It may seem as strange in Medicine that some Doctors should only prescribe vegetables and Galenical physick, perfectly hating chemistry, and that others, wholly inclined to novelty, should refuse all Medicines that are not chymically prepared.

Both parties (in mine opinion) are swayed more by fancy than by reason; for I suppose it absolutely necessary to study first your ancient, dogmatical Medicine, both as to the speculative and the practical part, and to correct the faults as we have already pointed in the first, second and third qualities; and the same course is to be taken in chymistry, so that they be without suspicion and deceit; and first we will begin with the old and proceed to the new.

We have sufficiently proved that there are occult properties and specific virtues in simplex, as no learned Galenist ever denied; who have also confessed that these did not work from their qualities or degrees, but their natures, to mitigate symptoms, take away the cause of the disease and to enthronize health in man's body.

If this be true, why are not physicians more careful in gathering and rightly understanding the nature of simplex? Fernelius in his book De abditis rerum caussi, saith that this specific virtue, which he calls the form, lies hid in every part of a simple and is diffused throughout all the elements. Hence if by chymistry water is drawn off, oil is extracted and salt made out of the ashes, each of these, the water, oil and salt, hath the specifical virtues of the simples; but I suppose one not so much as another, yet all joined together are perfect and compleat.

These things being laid down and confirmed, we must confess that the outward, tangible body of any simple, that may be beaten, cut, sifted, boiled, mingled with any other, to be the bark, the carcass and habitation of the specific quality, which is the pith, the Soul, the householder. And now what shall we say of our common preparations in apothecaries' shops, which have good and bad, nay most corrupt in them? Would not all laugh him to scorn who being commanded to call a master out of his house, will needs have the house along too? That cannot use the birds unless the nest be an ingredient, that cannot eat oysters unless he may also devour the shells? But the apothecaries think this lawful enough, because they can do no better. These Occult qualities, indeed, are so subtile that they make an easy escape unless they be narrowly watched and with a great skill housed or incorporated. Camphor loseth its strength unless it be cherished with flax seed. Rhubarb is preserved by wax and the Spirits of Wine. The Salt of goats' blood does evaporate if it be not close stopped in glasses.

What shall we then say of these specifical qualities separated from their bodies? Will not they return to their first principles? For who can separate the quality of burning from the fire? the quality of moistening from the

Water? But if this be impossible in simple bodies, how much more difficult in compound?

I could, therefore, wish that Medicines were used which were lawful, possible and reasonable, that laying aside ostentation and pride truth might flourish.

Perhaps we might allow of Syrups, Juleps, Conserves did not that great quantity of Sugar clog the natural operation of the Simple. Perhaps we might approve of Electuaries, Opiates, Antidotes, unless the multitude of Simples confusedly put together did hinder, if not totally extinguish the true virtue. Perhaps pills and all bitter, sour, sharp, stinking Medicines are good; but yet they destroy appetite, cause loathsomeness, that a patient had better endure the disease than the remedy. If bitterness, sourness, sharpness and an ill savour are the specifical qualities, they should be rather checked than let loose, and indeed they are but handmaids to their Mistress, but subservient to the Specifical Quality and the true difference is discovered by Chymistry, for it separates the impure parts from the pure if rightly used. Yet mistake not, we say not that chymical preparations are altogether spiritual and without any body, but are more piercing and subtile, more defecated than gross bodies made more heavy by a great quantity of Sugar, so that they are not free and at liberty to act and play their parts.

By this time you may see the folly and madness of those who hate chymistry, which ought to be used, but with care and judgement; for it is not the part of a physician to burn, lance, cauterize and to take away the cause of the disease by weakening the patient and endangering of his life, but symptoms must be abated, nature restored and comforted by safe cordials. One Archagatus was the first chirugeon that came to Rome and was honourably received; but coming to use lancing and burning he was thought rather an hangman; and for the like cause at one time all physicians were banished [from] Rome. One Charmis, a physician, condemning the judgement of his predecessors, set up new inventions of his own and commanded his patients in frost and snow to bathe in cold water as Pliny reports; who saith also that he hath seen old men sit freezing by his direction. Acesias about to cure the gout, looked more to the disease than pain, which be neglect increased, whence the proverb had its original, Acesias medicatus est, as Erasmus hath it, when the condition grows worse, Acesia his cure.

It is clear enough from what hath been delivered that Nature is best satisfied when profitable and wholesome Medicines are applied. Asclepiades, an intimate friend of Cn. Pompey, first showed the benefit of wine to sick persons, recovering a man carried to his grave. He taught to maintain health by a moderate use of meat and drink, an exact care in exercise and much rubbing; he invented delightful and pleasing potions; he commanded bathing and for ease to his patients invented hanging beds that sleep might surprise them in such a careless posture. The same Pliny saith that Democritus was a physician, who in the cure of Considia, daughter to Consul Sereilius, did forbear harsh means and by the long and continual use of goats milk recovered her.

Agron, as Coelius reports, Lib. 13, cap. 22, was a physician at Athens, who, in a great plague, when many were infected, did only cause to be made great fires nigh to the place; and thus did Hippocrates, for which he was much honoured.

Whence we may learn that mild and gentle usage in a disease is more efficacious to the taking away of the cause and to healing the symptoms, than harsh and rugged dealing. The mariner doth [not] pray for a full gale many times to force him into his desired harbour, neither doth the traveller go in a direct line, yet both in the end attain their hopes. We read that Fabius, by delay conquered his enemy, so that it is a masterpiece of prudence well and naturally to deliberate and then to execute; yet the method of curing remains and the axioms are firm, viz.: if the cause be taken away, the effect ceaseth; if the disease is cured the symptoms do vanish and wear away.

But chymistry stores and supplies us with Medicines which are safe, pleasant and soon perform that for which they were intended: and others have abundantly set forth this in their writings, and therefore it will not be requisite to stand longer upon it.

Let us face about and view those who are mere chemists. These would be called young Theophrasts, affecting like their master a Divine title, which he neither had by his father nor mother, but assumed it to himself as most magnificent and glorious. But without all doubt he was a man of eminent and admirable knowledge in the Art of Physick, yet surely it would be worthily judged madness for his sake alone to forsake the Ancients and follow his new inventions.

It may seem an absurd thing for one to undertake to restore a very old man to his former strength, because Death it then approaching and every man at length must submit to his sceptre.

Is not the world now ancient and full of days and is it not folly to think of recovering and calling back its youth? Surely their new Medicine cannot revive the dying world, it may weaken it and hasten its end. Yet stay, I pray you, do not imagine that I do at present censure the excellent and plainly divine preparations of chemistry, but rather the persons who profess it, who make it their business to destroy but endeavour not to build, who trample on others to raise and exalt themselves; as Thessalus of old did, railing against all men who were not their followers. So Chrysippus, master to Eristratus, to gain pre-eminence, despised and changed Hippocrates. These and such like men are wont to promise much, but perform little; for we may certainly conclude, that although such persons may affect greatness, yet they shall never attain it by such indirect means. I would many of the Paracelsians did not too much conform to their Master's vices. If many late writings were scanned and their abuses and tart language against others left out, I doubt [not] their volumes would very much shrink. It were much better that diseases, the common enemies, were more looked after than private grudges amongst physicians themselves revenged. Brute beasts do bark and show their teeth and spit venom; a man's weapon is Reason, by which he should foil his adversaries.

As touching chemistry, we highly commend and admire those things in it which are good, but yet so as not to despise Galenical physic, which in some cases is as effectual. My own opinion is that each ought to be used in its proper place. Men are not mere Spirits, but corporeal substances and therefore need not Medicines exalted to their highest degree of perfection, as least in every grief applied to every person and to every part or member. There are some diseases, which, being hot and dry, are not to be cured by chymical prescriptions whose ingredients or preparations have the like qualities. In a commonwealth there is a merchant, there is a husbandman, but one ought not to supplant the other; so a prudent physician will make use of both as he sees occasion, the one for a countryman, the other for a delicate person; the one in a slight distempers, the other in dangerous cases; the one for pleasantness, the other for efficacy as necessity requires.

www.ingramcontent.com/pod-product-compliance
Lightning Source LLC
Chambersburg PA
CBHW071751090426
42738CB00011B/2644